THE BOY FROM
ZAREPHATH

The Boy from Zarephath

Books by Robertson Tirado

The Boy from Zarephath

Life and Times of Carlina La Salle

Horatio's Journey

Films by Robertson Tirado

Bill & Gaby

Horatio's Odyssey

The Lost Interview of Carlina La Salle

THE BOY FROM
ZAREPHATH

ROBERTSON TIRADO

The Boy from Zarephath

East 4th Productions LLC
Ridgewood NY

Certificate of Registration is on file at Washington DC Copyright Office

ISBN-13: 978-0-578-51380-5

THE BOY FROM
ZAREPHATH

The Boy from Zarephath

The Boy from Zarephath

The color purple, when it glistens in the wind, is a color you can taste and feel without the need to touch it.

There was a purple cloth—perhaps remnants of a flag—somehow attached to a majestic stone on the side of a cliff with the names of eleven kings etched upon it. It seemed bathed in royalty. That's what I saw, furrowing in a light breeze, just before I enlisted.

I enlisted in the battle simply so that I could have access to food. My faith is not as strong as my mother's had been; hers was unequivocal, as fixed and well-defined as the moon and stars. Her beauty and affection for strangers were blessings. I was never as strong. In hard times, such as a drought, I was never sure if I'd ever find another meal.

My name is Jonah. My birth date was in the middle of the eighth century before the birth of Christ, in the land between Damascus and Zarephath. When I was ten years old, a drought caused a scarcity of food, which tore through our family life like an unforgiving wildfire, a tidal wave, and a devastating earthquake all rolled into one. Do not mistake me for the Jonah who was swallowed by the whale; I'm not a biblical hero— just a fatherless boy raised by a widow of extraordinary resolve. Her name was Chava.

It is hard to remember my father. The memory of him bounces gently in my mind, like a floating timber drifts in and out of the shores of the Mediterranean Sea. I both loved and hated the sea. I would listen to friends and neighbors say how fortunate we were to live in the constant cool breeze of the sea. When the drought began, there were far fewer visitors to town, and fewer sweet dates, as well. Mother's face glowed with joy whenever she saw me content, which in my own mind, my own world, I was able to be. But as many of our neighbors moaned at night, her face grew dark shadows. She and I would huddle together on cold nights, and I would touch her face to try to smooth away those stressful shadows. I was too young to truly understand stress, but I now know that those shadows merely worked overtime to help protect me.

My mother loved my father. I clung to the stories she told about him. In my darker times, memories of him kept hope alive. He was a temperate man in an unforgiving world. He worked as a skilled carpenter and sailing rig inspector and oversaw the maritime maintenance crews. My father was always excited about how each ship was bigger and better than the one before it, and how each new vessel needed more men to help construct them. The ships required larger sails and stronger timber, and as a result my father would earn more money. One of the vessels he worked on had an array of doves carved into both its port and starboard sides, cascading with other doves, small to large, all the way to the bow. As a skilled carpenter, he also sketched the doves for the men who did the carving. Some days his drawings were scattered in our cramped living space—not just of ornamental doves, but also all types lighter, faster sailing vessels.

I remained nameless for the first few months of my life. Mother had a lot with which to deal. She was frustrated, and grew more so as time passed. One night I started to kick the footboard of my tiny bed. The bed was nearly flush against my father's worktable, which had a shelf above it with taxidermy doves, small sparrows and various tools of his trade. As my kicking grew more intense, the bed frame bumped the worktable so hard that it knocked all the taxidermy onto my sheets and all his tools onto the floor. My mother and father jumped out of their own bed, which was only about two meters away, and saw the lifeless doves on my chest. Mother checked my face and limbs, but saw no injuries. They were relieved. What's more, my smile was illuminated by the lingering dim glow from the oven. They deduced that I had had a dream that made me restless, and that the doves landing on my chest was testimony to that fact. My father was not a religious man; he believed only in decisive evidence that can lead to truth. He glanced at his work station; it was surrounded by sketches of doves, so he announced to my mother that my name would be Jonah, which means dove. So that's why my name is Jonah.

The Battle

I began my journey in Zarephath, going from caravan to caravan, and traded my skills as a carpenter for safe passage to Hana. At twenty three, I was still quite naive—though I do admit to a mature thirst for adventure. At Hana learned irrigation techniques. The town, on the banks of the Orontes River, is a hostile place, and that's where I enlisted. Mother warned me not to travel east, where the Assyrian army was building its force.

The final caravan took me to the armies of Que Cilicia, on the banks of the Orontes River, where my platoon was trained in archery with the intent to penetrate the armor of the Assyrians. The tales told by the generals made most of my fellow soldiers go mad (there were three hundred of us at the time); perhaps it was some sort of internal spark that insulated me from a fear of death. I trusted the God of Elijah, who had guided my mother, as well.

Perched on a piece of timber, I sat on the marshy banks of the river watching the Egyptians in the distance, who are allies of Que Cilicia. They exercised under the starry night sky with a thirst for battle. I tried to rest, but two generals argued loudly about their lack of qualified soldiers, equipment and skilled men to repair chariots and wagons.

"I am the son of Yosef and Chava," I yelled. "I traveled from Zarephath. We're all tired, all of us men, and we need you to get along so that you can develop the right strategies to lead us to victory. Trust yourselves!"

The moon passed overhead.

One of generals stood up on a boulder and addressed the three hundred men, most of whom were lying on the marshy grass.

"This man speaks from the belly," he said about me. He seemed proud to have me in his charge. I admit—I was also proud of myself for finding the right words and the strength to use them.

When morning came, that same general came over to me and asked my rank and abilities.

"I'm a carpenter," I told him, "and I irrigate my mother's small plot of land."

"What do you plant?" he asked.

"Flax and melon."

"How can you help our armies?"

"I am strong," I assured him. "May I speak freely?"

"You may."

I told the general to dig trenches by the Orontes River so wounded soldiers can be put on log boats and mended quickly from their battlefield wounds. The general nodded, then hastened away and yelled for all to hear:

"Start digging!"

The troops worked together and sang as if in a choir. We filled the air with our boldness. As we dug, I enjoyed some of the sweetest sounds I've ever heard.

I looked at my hands and saw the hands of a little boy who knew what drought was, whose mother filled his head with comforting words.

At times, people cursed my mother for sheltering the man who many of them believed caused the drought. His name was Elijah. We knew him well. I would run to the door when he came from his ministry, as others wailed nearby. Elijah provided for us like a father. He told us stories about a powerful God who spoke to him. He said his God had directed him to us.

"Is he Baal?" I asked.

Elijah laughed so loudly that my mother ran in from milling flour in the kitchen. "It's all right,

Chava," he assured her. "Jonah is merely having fun hurting my belly by making me laugh."

Those were the best memories—when our home was full of laughter.

The men from Que Cilicia were comprised of slaves, hired archers, and foreigners such as myself. In truth, I didn't have faith in this army. The Assyrians, by contrast, had a skilled army and three manned chariots. When we dug trenches, the river receded as the banks absorbed into the clay. Near me, some men used the clay to make bricks for small fire pits. Maybe it was my youth, but something contributed by my ability to ignore fear. Although I never participated in battle, I understood every breath could be my last.

Often I thought of mother and my younger brother. He was born when I was fifteen years old. It was a pleasure to have him around, especially when so many children my age moved away, which happened quite often. His hair was red and curly, his complexion lighter than mine, his hands large. Mother said he would be a good farmer one day. By the time he was two-and-a-half he was able to read.

I had a stepfather at that time, and he did not talk very much. He was always tired. Indeed, most of the men in our city were exhausted if they couldn't afford a beast of burden to do some work for them. Animals helped our farmers speed up the harvest. But there weren't many animals to be had. Also, to earn steady income, many of the men would journey for several months to distant lands. Our own family, in fact, traveled from place to place after my father passed away. That's when Elijah lived with us. Mother made extra income from baking bread, although she was able to sell it just once a week.

Still, life was joyful, particularly when there was a full moon. My brother and I would stay up those nights and watch from outside. Later, whenever I glanced at the men from Que Cilicia, I realized how many of them seemed traumatized by life. But all men look to the heavens for faith, even if their faith isn't as strong as Elijah's. To be sure, Elijah's God is not favored by King Ahab, our ruler. That's the way it had always been. King Ahab ruled us and we assembled to keep him sovereign by showing him our strength in numbers and the passion of our devotion. After the drought and execution of Baal's prophets, mother whispered to me about Elijah's God. She knew that his God was a protector of ordinary people like us.

My Brother

The drought changed mother. When she was pregnant with my brother she would make me listen to him moving around in her womb and ask me what name we should give him. The first thing that came to mind was Elijah, so that's what I said. It was the first time I saw my mother weep. I remember the elder Elijah, with his coarse beard and the wrinkles near his eyes, and the skin that glowed, not from the sun, but from something else entirely.

When my brother was born, our neighbors made us a modest feast. We were very happy. But as food became more plentiful, we heard of men leaving for battle. Food would be needed for the war; there would less for those left behind.

That's what filled my mind once I went to battle. Surrounded by strangers, I missed my home terribly. Two weeks after I left Zarephath I vowed to return, I had seen mothers and younger brothers suffer, so I decided to write a letter home.

If, as planned, the army was to cross the river and meet the armies of Byblos, the men, most of whom were eunuchs, were set to fortify the Eastern banks with mud. A eunuch was a deserter of the Assyrian empire. One in particular had tremendous knowledge of the bow. He told me he had served in the court of King Shalmaneser III. We spoke until the sun cooled and he warned me about the Assyrians' merciless raids and conquering campaigns. Still, I refused to be afraid.

The Letter

"First, I miss you very much," I wrote to my mother. "Today I am resting near the Orontes River, after a long three days of preparing for war with King Shalmaneser III. I know that you warned me of great peril in this endeavor, this conflict—but I write with complete confidence that I will reunite with you before too long. An unfortunate wave of convoys steered me to the armies of Que Cilicia. As you already must know, our King is part of an eleven king front preparing for battle with Shalmaneser III, a bully of a King, to be sure—what I'd call the Bully King of the Assyrians.

"I speak from the heart, mother, when I talk about my desire to have a wife and children one day. This journey brought along with it much loneliness and has hindered my happiness, even though I spoke to the God of Elijah during my travels. I am glad that I did, but I must tell you that it still was not enough to fill the void. Being part of this campaign to defend our home, rather than being pushed into the sea, will ensure a better life for you and for your other son, my brother.

"I am surrounded by good men, some of the bravest, some who remember the drought when I was a boy. Many question how we were able to survive it. I keep silent about our special house guest who brought about the salvation. Our rugged life here is filled with salty breezes and quiet nights. I find myself thinking of roasted vegetables and our garden filled with blue flax.

"When I return, I will make time to discover my father's shipbuilding talents for myself. Some of it was passed on to me, and of that I am pleased and proud. Our hearts are aligned, mother, and my faith is aligned with your example. This is the reason I have no fear in this strange land. There are things that I have never seen. There is an abundance of manpower that accomplishes so much in so little time. Relying upon your examples keeps me focused. This letter is not meant to cause you more anxiety. I urge you to read between the lines. This letter is intended to strengthen you spirit while your older son presses forth and your younger one remains safe and happy."

Disguised

Some men are fearful of the war and change their attire to appear as common folk, or they move away to blend in with other cultures to avoid the battles and the inevitable tragedies that follow. We heard of tribes being captured by the Assyrian army to the North, and we heard of eunuchs quarreling and meditating. It is indeed an odd scene.

On our third day of digging, the trench was more than sixty cubic meters long and one cubic meter deep. As I stood in the mud I was able to see the dim reflection of my curly hair, which had grown longer. My reflection reminded me of my mother; she was reflected in my light golden eyes. My garments, wrapped loosely around my waist, would never protect me well in battle. But I still had faith, and mental strength.

For most men, when their homes are burned to the ground, they take up the sword and the bow and vow to defend their families and possessions. I learned from the stories of my comrades, whose minds are fresh with battle and whose eyes are weary with hopelessness, that some of them fought in the mountains and some battled on the shores of the Euphrates. They told of a river that turned red and a merciless Assyrian soldier who disguised himself with a wrap of whale blubber.

One of the tales—one of the hardest to comprehend—was about a battle five years earlier, at the Euphrates River. Two soldiers confirmed the accuracy of the story. They were from Bit-Adini and spoke of magic in the water as they fled the annihilation of their entire army from all fronts. Bit-Adini shared both sides of the Euphrates River as Adini was attacked first by Shalmaneser III. Those of the eastern Bit-Adini fleet of ships rolled up their sails so that the archers' arrows would not set fire to them. One soldier said he was on a small boat, one of three that were tethered to a larger ship carrying one hundred fifty men. The small boats worked as a team, with enough momentum to sail beside the large ships on their way to the shores of Adini. A total of six ships maneuvered the same way, with three small boats and six men with oars. As we got closer to the Assyrian onslaught, from the distance one of the small boats was overtaken by Assyrian soldiers from the abyss of the Euphrates River.

From this abyss the reptilian Assyrians were able to maneuver like sea creatures. Just how, I can't explain. Wobbly ankles made the sailors easy prey for execution. One by one, each boat capsized.

"We were swimming to the larger vessel," said the man from Bit-Adini.

"How did you survive?" I asked.

"The momentum of my ship put us in the direct aim of the Assyrian battering rams, the largest battering rams I ever saw."

"But the reptilian Assyrian?"

"A battering ram full of hot coals," he explained, "was jammed into the ship and ignited it into flames, forcing me to jump into the Euphrates."

The man from Bit-Adini lifted his apron to show me his second-degree burn marks. "I am no coward," he asserted. "We were the only survivors."

I tried to understand their pain. With all this war, I wondered, how did Shalmaneser attain riches if everything he touches is made into ashes?

We walked to where some people were preparing dinner. The butcher showed us where the carcasses were kept. The man from Bit-Adini grabbed a bloody lung; the tissue glowed from the blaze of the

19

campfire. He put his mouth to its large opening and blew into it until it expanded with enough air to fill ten liters.

"This is how the reptilian Assyrian breathed under the Euphrates," I said.

"Yes, our enemies are very clever," he responded. "Will we survive?"

"I believe *we* will, but our kingdoms, our tribes, will not."

"How do you know?" the Bit-Adini man asked.

"We all know pain, yet survived. We all learned how to free our minds from Shalmaneser."

"But we have many kingdoms ready to take down Shalmaneser, yet you say we will not survive?"

"Look at the fallen tribes and kingdoms to the west, wiped from time," I said. "The men here are but a handful of survivors. Their minds are psychologically fragile—complete wrecks. We need more than courage, weapons and muscle."

"So what do we need?" asked the man from Bit-Adini.

"To live again," I said.

Both replied with surprise, and in unison:

"What?"

"Those souls who perished along the Euphrates, those who suffered slow deaths in my city of drought and famine."

The Boy from Zarephath

The man from Bit-Adini walked away in disgust. I tamped down my rant of hope and held back my enthusiasm. Our world was as harsh as the very sand beneath our sandals. But I believed there could be hope in all of it, a spirit of second chances.

Kings

Drought and famine burdened us. We hoped this battle would free us. Some successfully fought a decade ago in Damascus, when they pushed back the Assyrian army, but now the Assyrians have stronger armor and more chariots and arrows of ingenious design. When the arrows missed their targets they broke apart, which prevented the enemy from reusing them. Razzia is what most feared, but in the distance smoke rose ominously, and there were reports of a league led by King Adadidri of Damascus with more than a thousand chariots. The irony was that King Ahab had fought against Damascus, and now we were gathered to battle Shalmaneser III as a league united against them. It was a horror to know that so many resources were needed to do battle with them. The King of Que and the Kings of Irkana and Adunuba joined us, and behind them were the armies of King Hamath. They knew the Orontes region and they knew the river well. Therefore, the tribe settled there to defend the land. Hamath had two hundred more chariots than we had, and well over ten thousand men. We marched that afternoon and funneled to the Orontes River. It felt like a trap—either for us or for them, in fact--because the earth trembled constantly, not with earthquakes, but with the trembling conversion of the armies of Arvad, Ushana and Musri.

The morning sun was gentle, and the air thick with sweat. I moved away from the river to dry my sandals. The skin of the men was the color of clay and sand. My mind drifted to the savagery of my homeland. When I was a boy, Elijah had whispered to me to keep hope eternally alive. I did not understand well at the time, but now, here by the riverbank, as we marched, I understood it much better. One of the men, just to my left, handed me a spear.

"What is your name?" he asked.

"Jonah, from Zarephath," I responded.

"What King do you represent?"

"King of Que and King Ahab."

"This man is magnificent," he said. "He fights for two kings. Stay between us in battle."

I was mentally prepared. I knew my mother and my brother needed me, and I needed them. That's what added to my resolve to survive the war. The thought crossed my mind how one man's actions can lead to so much suffering. Ahab's ruthless leadership brought death and shame, and gave men like Shalmaneser the courage and will to test the sovereignty of the eleven kings.

As I live on I realize that the kings have shown neither valor nor a true concern for their people. It is a shame that we have been forced to be human shields for their right to live in luxury.

We all know this. But people huddled in cities gave the illusion of security, even though many had been sacked by the Assyrians. The leaders chose gluttony over humanity.

Eleven kings, in my opinion, were slow to protect our neighbors. Had they worked together from the beginning, Shalmaneser might have retreated. From what I had heard from some of the men in my camp, even if we had surrendered to Shalmaneser, our lives would not have been spared. Villages such as Aribua and Lubarna, whose people kneeled to the Assyrians, were wiped out. Everyone was slaughtered. So we simply *had* to fight the battle. We had to trust ourselves, our faiths, and our plans. It was compulsory for us to put cowardice and ignorance aside—and fight.

The Battle at Qarqar

Through the soft blades of tall grass, three hundred men knelt and rubbed dirt on the tips of their weapons. Our enemies were in the distance, and the smell of death was in the air. The camels who carried or supplies were coated with the mud of the Orontes River. The sounds of metal belts and buckles on the beasts of burden were the only sounds passing though the huddled web of men. In moments, strangers become comrades. Nearby, a young man pointed to his scarred chest, on which was branded the letters YAM.

"I am Jonah," I whispered to the young man.

"My name is U," he said.

He smiled without opening his mouth. U told me—and several soldiers around me—to focus on the men a half mile away on horses; there were eleven of them, one representing each of the kings.

"I can see the commander for Ahab," U said. "What tribe do you fight for?"

"Que," I answered. "My mother, brother and I live in Zarephath."

"From what I heard, King Ahab is a merciless leader," he continued. "I understand why you defected to Que."

I looked to the heavens. The sun melted our backs. How many suns have set on my life, I silently wondered. In my mind I mulled over the importance of this battle. I knew there was a clear threat to all who lived east of the Orontes River. Those who I loved were there, and we had a chance to stop Shalmaneser.

The Boy from Zarephath

The armies of the eleven kingdoms stretched two-and-a-half kilometers along the Orontes River. We were at the southernmost point with Que, with five hundred men on the ground. Ahab's foot infantry numbered ten thousand, with two thousand chariots, in addition to eunuchs and slaves. Legend had it that they possessed the strongest, fastest, most agile chariots in the kingdom. Only the Assyrian armies came close to the skills of the Hamath, who had seven hundred horses. While I dug the trench I overheard all these facts, numbers, observations and speculations of the armies and the battles. Twenty thousand men here; twelve hundred chariots there; over a thousand horsemen; the combined eleven-thousand-man force of three small kingdoms, Irkana, Musri and Shiana, with only a few chariot scouts numbering between twenty and thirty; King Matinuba'li's renown for having taken part in the battles; Arvad and Ushana providing a group of two hundred men that, nevertheless, was considered the mightiest army.... So many numbers, so many facts, so many tales, so much to comprehend and consider...

All told, there was confidence in numbers, and the smell of war approached.

If the kings had been truly united before this battle at Qarqar, the outcome would have been different. But they fought with each other.

The Boy from Zarephath

What I learned from Elijah was that his God remembers those who suffer. I had seen it firsthand as a boy at the worship of Baal. The prophets did not stop the drought and famine. Some days I found myself beating my chest because I knew my faith should be stronger. The horizon is as true as the morning sun and the crashing waves of the sea. Elijah's God brought victory to our home. Elijah visited the chambers of kings, came eye to eye with evil, was hunted by squads—but chose us to help. His spirit glowed in our home. I slept well when Elijah stayed with us.

But back to the reality of war, two man on a chariot from Gindibu, covered in full bronze, with iron breast plates covering their hearts, moved past us and shouted a single word: "Stand!" Men from Que saluted. We stood and stretched as far as the horizon, eight men deep, ready to face an enemy with pinpoint ambition to make it to the Mediterranean Sea.

"What is my first tactic in battle?" I asked U

He looked at me with an unpleasant squint, grunted, and said,

"Men are natural killers. No training is needed."

"I will not take a life," I asserted.

"So you will die."

U grabbed me.

"You speak of a brother and of a mother," he said. "We are at the end."

I nodded.

"You are brave, Jonah," he continued. "You are different. I need to be by your side. Follow us and run between two chariots. They will clear a path for the fastest runners. Our goal is to penetrate their first line and set ablaze their camps and their food supply."

"How do you know this?"

"I heard from some of the men who survived the Assyrian ransacking that their weaknesses are no different from anyone else's. They need food to fight another day. We may be the first to perish."

"We will not perish!"

The sun reached the hour before its highest point in the sky. We were no longer hidden in the shadows. Our enemies were in plain sight. So many of us were weathered by war. But I felt no fear as I prayed to the God of Elijah as he once instructed me to do. Mother and I had not known what prayer was, or how to do it. One time at dinner Elijah asked us a few questions.

"The beasts of burden tame the land, the birds sing in the morning and awaken the silent," he said. Mother and I nodded, but didn't understand what he was leading to. Then he asked, "Do sea creatures thank the crashing waves or the bee its morning blossom? They do in silence. Their vibrations give praise, and then nourishment to us, who are made in God's image." Mother steadfastly agreed with his words.

The Boy from Zarephath

In the distance came the cry of a thousand men. It was the cry of battle, along with the stomping of feet.

"This is it, Jonah," said U.

"May the God of Elijah protect us both," my friend.

Our center stronghold had been attacked. I stood between the chariots. U was behind me. I charged on foot and heard the whoosh of spears from the ships on the Orontes River. The flaming spears illuminated our path to a wall of Assyrian men. My heart beat heavy as we got closer. The chariots sped into the wall of spears, flipping their chariots, seconds from defeat.

"Jonah, the cavalry!" U yelled toward me.

The Egyptians, flanked by a thousand camels, trampled the Assyrian forces. U and I continued to charge on foot as the camels penetrated the southern blockade. We jumped over the carnage and yelled with all our strength to the wind. The Arabian league was now far in the distance, and we were alone. But cries of savagery could still be heard, We looked at each other, completely out of breath and panting.

"Jonah, the camels!"

A hundred men on camels started to head to us.

"U, let's go!"

The Arabians were coming at full speed to finish the job. The earth pounded, the beasts snorted heavily. Some of the Assyrians under their mangled armor pushed away to get a better stance at the charging league. Over two dozen of them raised their spears and took aim at us. U and I raised our shields to defect penetration of our softer metal armor. I was able to smell the breath of the camels. We tasted victory.

King Ahab

Those in the league told hostile stories about Ahab. I believe that many of the stories are true.

When I was a boy in Zarephath, I remember mother and Elijah talking at dinner about Ahab, but they made me leave the room because some of the stories of which they spoke were unfit for my youthful ears. But I did catch snippets from time to time.

Elijah's bedroom was in the pantry on the ground floor of our home. Mother had cleared the space of all of my father's shipbuilding instruments. It was a cleansing of sorts. Indeed, it was a pleasure to see Elijah in the mornings, for we were common folk who had a very important person living with us.

On one occasion, he failed to come home for two days. We didn't know it at the time, but he was quarreling with the king. How, mother wondered at the time, did a man of such modest means make his way to speak with Ahab? Also, the king's wife Jezebel hated men like Elijah. To her he was a mysterious old man who had more courage than most of the men in the army. What did Elijah talk about in Ahab's palace? I will never know. But just the thought of it opened my mind—my mother's, too—into a reality beyond our natural world.

So as I ran into battle, I paused with memories of Elijah's stories, even his mannerisms, such as his gentle snoring, which when I was boy hit my ears with affection as if it were a real father snoring close by.

Life was a contrast—a contrast between the peaceful Elijah and the hostile environment around us, a contrast between King Ahab's victories and the suffering of our region. As the drought and famine grew more intense, our king fought Benhadad. Many kingdoms took advantage of Ahab's weakened army. One cannot flee the battlefield. Sooner or later we all have our feet stuck in. How do I know this? Because mother fled the southern plains of Damascus. She put me on her back when I grew tired of walking. She stopped at Zarephath and it became our home. I was seven years old.

From my point of view, many cities are cursed. As soon as they build, they are destroyed. Mother's decision to stay in Zarephath was a wise one, despite the famine, for we were spared the wrath of the Assyrian armies.

The Boy from Zarephath

It was always a hostile place, even when I was a boy. Baal recruits would make frequent visits to our sector, and mother would present herself outside our door before they knocked. She would not say much, but something in her eyes made them back away. Some nights, the inner parts of the city would illuminate from Baal celebrations. In this hostile environment, mother resisted its lure; her faith protected those closest to her.

As a grown man, my faith is based on her example, especially her trust in Elijah. Yes, he was a stranger, and I never really understood mother's core beliefs. I did not understand it—but I accepted it.

In the Que tribe of warriors, some looked at me as if I was different from them. One asked, "How do you speak so well?" Said another, "Why does your posture seem to lack suffering from the fields?" Most of the men lived through tragedy. So had I, of course, but mother's wise choices and prudence protected me from terrifying experiences, both physical and emotional. Living under the rule of King Ahab was a curse and a blessing at once. Constant wars protected our home from the slaughter of the Assyrians.

During the famine, mother and I were sustained. Sometimes it seemed like a miracle.

Home

Our home in Zarephath was larger than the home of my birth father. My room was above the kitchen, and the aroma of lamb stew and roasted vegetables was a delightful treat once a year. Mother built relationships with local merchants and traded her culinary services for meals, rent and lamp oil. Sometimes I would sit upon the top step outside and watch mother spin wheat and oil into delicacies. As she squatted over the dusty earth, the sizzle of frying oil always made my hunger pangs flare in anticipation. Sometimes it was lonely; other times there were the happy sounds of newborn babies nearby. Mother would wake early and tend to our small garden. As drought and famine swept over us, we did not need the sound of crying babies to put us to sleep; hunger did the trick.

Just days into the drought, strangers knocked at our door asking for some of the few items we grew in our garden. Mother was firm; she told each visitor our supply never matured, making human consumption impractical. She warned me to refrain from answering the door when she searched for work and food. I remember the time a letter was slipped under our front door. I was in the kitchen, so I went upstairs to my room where the small window looked directly over the door. I dragged over a stool so that I could reach the latch holding the shutters closed. It was noon, and hot outside, and when I peeked outside I saw a small boy, about my age. He moved slightly away from the door, and that drew my attention away toward the side of the house, where I saw two beggars hiding. Slowly I drew my head back into the room, shuffled over to my bed, and stood perfectly still. It was a dangerous time, a desperate time.

As the days became even more desperate, mother would share survival strategies with me. We would prepare meals in such a way to cut cooking time in half so that our neighbors would be less inclined to notice. She would prop me up on the second floor window ledge and show how many people watched to see if smoke came from our chimney. But in this difficult time she somehow found flour and dates. Her favorite color was red, so she covered her head with red scarves, which always brightened the mood at home. Mother moved her bed to the front door at night to ensure that no one would pry it open. On some days I would awaken and sit on the top step to stare at mother, as if to watch her spirit ward off all dangers. She knew how to make me laugh. With her long nails she would tickle my belly. One time I helped her dye another head scarf red. Our hands were red for over a week! I was young and water was plentiful. We moved to Zarephath when I was seven. It was only later on that I realized how for most of her life she had carried

The Boy from Zarephath

a knot of guilt—guilt about my father dying, guilt about moving to a land plagued by famine... She thought of herself as a foolish woman. Even though her faith was tested and proven time and time again and she received blessings from God, she still fought inner battles.

My mother did not wear shame. She was open to new thoughts and experiences. She gave me insights to the man who saved our lives when I was ten. She believed she had run away from problems in the past, but when we moved to Zarephath she decided to open herself to new paths of thought. Being alone with a son, she never had enough strength to fight every battle. Some things she had to let unfold naturally.

As my travels continued, mother's example of letting things unfold naturally, to learn from past experiences, to believe in what you do not understand, took me from the heart of battle back to the center of reality.

Home is where people care for you, where you become familiar with all that can hurt you or bring you joy. Mother made our home welcoming to all strangers. Elijah and my two companions became part of my home. While neither blood relatives nor spiritual affiliates, they were nevertheless made one with me through shared experience and trust. A home cannot stand without trust. It is a bond that ties. It is stronger than blood and religion. My mother and Elijah were not joined by the same faith or a distant relative; instead, it was an inner bond of compassion and conviction.

Why did I go back to Elijah when he only spent half a year in our home? Because at the hardest time in our life, we were happy. Mother was at ease when Elijah stayed with us. She told me the very first words he uttered were these:

"1 Kings 17: 10 & 11. So he arose and went to Zarephath; and when he came to the gate of the city, behold, a widow was there gathering sticks: and he called to her, and said, Fetch me, I pray thee, a little water in a vessel, that I may drink. And as she was going to fetch it, he called to her, and said, Bring me, I pray thee, a morsel of bread in thy hand."

Undoubtedly, what God noticed, what made him choose, was my mother's interaction with Elijah and her willingness to open her heart in the most troublesome of times .She was a woman who gathered sticks, who was without a husband. It was her humility that save us all.

Shalmaneser

As I've said, my youth led me to the battlefield. I thought I could outsmart a hostile region. I knew quite well that the Assyrian raids pillaged Argana, and I was aware of the reports that told of Hamath turning to ash. The caravan I rode with was part of the Hamath armies, and they sought revenge. Many refugees of battle were more dangerous to themselves than to others, as they knew all they had lost and were more than willing to sacrifice their souls. The name Shalmaneser was feared since I was a boy, but Shalmaneser III, from his advances over mountains and rivers, left charred cities in his wake. It was said that law and order was his goal. But when a city or a tribe refused to give tribute, Shalmaneser made a great assault that compelled nearly every other tribe that witnessed the assault to offer tributes. I learned some of these things from Luhuti, who worshipped the god Hadad, who once planted and timbered cedar trees and was forced to pay taxes with all of his inventory.

I asked him, "Your name is just like the city."

"Yes," he replied. "I am the last born of seventeen, so my parents named me after the city from which our grandparents came."

Luhuti was part of the caravan with which I traveled. Lying there in the wagon he would mumble to the heavens. When we met with the Que armies his mumbling became more intense, Luhuti recognized my interest and told me of his god Hadad, the bringer of rain and storms. So l asked him if his god granted his prayers.

"Yes," he acknowledged.

The Boy from Zarephath

While traveling to Que he told of giving tribute to Hadad and all the good his family enjoyed from their worship. He said he had many carved stone gods and tangible artifacts.

"My god wears a bulled headdress and carries a thunderbolt," he explained.

"My god is invisible," I responded. "My faith is not fully developed. There isn't anything tangible in my worship."

"I do not understand."

"My worship is the worship of the invisible."

"You are silent in your worship?" he asked.

"An old man named Elijah lived with my mother and me for a few years. I worship his God."

"Who is this invisible God?" Luhuti asked, now even more curious.

"YHWH."

"I have never heard of YHWH."

"My mother trusted YHWH without fully understanding, but he was my protector in the horrors of drought and famine."

"I'll remember Elijah and YHWH in battle," Luhuti called out. "We need all the protection we can get."

Reborn

I remembered a feast we had had when I was ten years old. Our small table made the banquet look larger than it really was. Every ingredient was baked slow and cooked with love. At the table was mother, her face glowing like never before. Elijah and I sat at the table watching her create miracles of aroma. The kindling fire made some neighbors peek through the windows. Some of them shouted "Chava, what are you cooking?" Mother paid no attention to them, but simply hummed while she put three bowls full of flavorful garden vegetables and a sliver of lamb onto the table. Before we ate, we prayed and gave thanks.

I needed to remember those moments. There is no turning back time in the mud of war. There on the horizon awaited our fate. That's why memories were so important. I hoped the God of Elijah would stop this carnage, much of which was brought upon by ourselves. Worshiping strange gods, sacrificing everything to Baal, using limited resources to construct objects or trinkets to a silent God while many starved... all of this was difficult to understand. In a world like ours, many gave up on the God of Israel after the drought. Worship and a love for the God of Noah and Moses dried up like the rivers. One can have pity on the decisions many had made, since they were driven to desperation and to an alternative to their spiritual needs.

One would think our small, unimportant speck in the sand with so many in need of a savior could be as blessed as we. But then to cross paths with Elijah, God directed him to seek a widow, and together they showed an immediate compassion to one another. This stranger, Elijah, unrelated to our family, came to the rescue, whether on the battlefield or in the marketplace. Anyone with a pure heart can be a great ally.

I did not know the gravity of Elijah's reach, but I will always remember his rosy cheeks when he smiled at me at the conclusion of mother's feast. Mother relied on Elijah to provide food. She never took it for granted that it would always be there. But because of mother's inventiveness as a widow, rumors spread that we were secretly wealthy from the assets of my father's trade.

During the brief time that Elijah stayed with us, our home repelled the dark energy and the malevolent spells seemingly cast by some. Those who practiced the dark arts knew to avoid him, knowing how he was hated by Ahab for causing the drought. Even so, whispers went out that a powerful prophet was staying in the house of the widow and her son. Many children died from the famine; I was one of the fortunate few from Zarephath who not only survived, but remained healthy. If not for the food, which I attribute to a miracle from God, I would not have been here to defend my homeland.

It was U who said that his father lived in Zarephath in the year 859.

"We are the same age, Jonah" he said to me. "My father never spoke of miracles or foolish tales, but he told a story I will never forget."

Several of us asked U about the story.

"A boy raised from the dead," he began.

"Stop with false hope and lies," one of the men said as we prepared for battle.

"Father said the boy was fatherless, raised by his mother," said U.

"What does that story mean to you?" I asked. "Why do you remember it?"

"I told this story many times. If only I can find him some day."

"When you find him, what will you say to him?"

"There are many children's stories that parents tell, but this one gives me hope—always has, all through my teenage years. It means we are not just mosquitoes, not just forgotten gnats."

"Is your father still alive?" I asked.

"Yes, but very ill."

"Does that story gives you hope now?"

The Boy from Zarephath

"Whatever morsel of strength I need I gather through experience and wisdom," he insisted.

"So that story about the boy from Zarephath is real to you?"

"Again, yes, Jonah! I remember when he came home that week he was different. Most of the time he was tired from traveling and hardly talked—he just ate and slept. It was a hard life. Even though we lived in a safe part of the city, father still worried about our safety. I was the middle child, with a older sister and a younger brother. Father had to work extra hard because of a gambling debt."

U looked at me and for a moment seemed upset when he mentioned the gambling debt.

"This particular night," he continued, "father came home with so much vigor that he woke us all up and told us to come down for gifts. Mother was glowing. It was a part of him that she had not much seen in recent months. The three of us stood in rapt attention as father kissed us and handed us our gifts."

U showed me a small stone pendant that was hidden under his top and said it was the gift his father had given him that night.

"We each got a different gift that reflected his love for us. It was as if he had a boost of fatherly love and basic humanity. He hugged us tightly and kissed us good night."

The Boy from Zarephath

"So what about the boy?" I asked gently so that I would not undermine his pleasant memory.

"Just before our city was burned to the ground, mother, in her frail state, reminded me of the time my father had given us those gifts."

A man several meters away barked at us to keep. So U continued in a whisper.

"That week, my father stayed in Zarephath," U continued in a low voice. "In those days, my father did what he could to pay his gambling debts. He heard there were a few souls with a bounty on their heads in Zarephath. One person who he sought out was an enemy of King Ahab, an elderly man who took up residence with a widow and her son. This foreigner, it seems, had a large bounty on his head—one of the largest. My father trapped this man by climbing onto the roof of a neighboring house where he could get a good look at him. While on the roof, he had a clear view inside the second-floor bedroom. As my father hid behind the neighbor's chimney, he witnessed a young boy lying in his bed while his mother put wet cloths on his forehead. The elderly man came upstairs to the bedroom. He and the women started to quarrel. He told her to leave him and the boy alone. From my father's vantage point, he was able to see that the boy wasn't sick; he was dead."

U became very emotional while he continued to tell the story.

The Boy from Zarephath

"What happened then changed the course of my father's life forever," he said—and then quoted 1 Kings 17-24:

And it came to pass after these things that the son of the woman, the mistress of the house, fell sick; and his sickness was so sore, that there was no breath left in him. And she said unto Elijah, What have I to do with thee, O thou man of God? Thou art come unto me to bring my sin to remembrance, and to slay my son! And he said unto her, Give me thy son. And he took him out of her bosom, and carried him up into the chamber, where he abode, and laid him upon his own bed. And he cried unto Jehovah, and said, O Jehovah my God, hast thou also brought evil upon the widow with whom I sojourn, by slaying her son? And he stretched himself upon the child three times, and cried unto Jehovah, and said, O Jehovah my God, I pray thee, let this child's soul come into him again. And Jehovah hearkened unto the voice of Elijah; and the soul of the child came into him again, and he revived. And Elijah took the child, and brought him down out of the chamber into the house, and delivered him unto his mother; and Elijah said, See, thy son liveth. And the woman said to Elijah, Now I know that thou art a man of God, and that the word of Jehovah in thy mouth is truth.

U then went into further detail about his father.

"Life," he said, "was hard on all of us, and for my father, who was supporting a large family. His heart grew callous. A sandstorm in his mind clogged all reason and civility. At times he was hard on all of us. Maybe I am still alive today because of his rigid, unforgiving ways, but after that night, doing things in secret and staying away from home for long periods of time became a distant memory in our household."

"Some people never change. He did," said Al Biqa, a man with long hair and a sturdy expression.

"Some men are naturally so stubborn that we can hardly blame them," I acknowledged. "But if someone is willing to soften their heart because of a new experience, well, then..." I left the sentence unfinished. Everyone knew what I meant.

"Even when his financial opportunities dried up, father handled it differently than before he saw the boy awakened by the hand of the prophet Elijah."

Al Biqa asked, "I never heard of this prophet Elijah. Do you know anything about him?"

"Father spoke more about the boy than the old man," U said. "But he was not just a prophet. Jezebel wanted him dead. Some said he was the cause of a great famine in Israel."

"Jonah," Al Biqa commented, "you suddenly became quiet."

"They were hard times," I said. "There was a lot of suffering. We lost many neighbors who were the same age as I."

"How did you and you mother survive?" asked Al Biqa.

"I do not want to talk about it. My mother did what she had to do."

"I understand" he said softly.

U spoke up once again. "May the prophet Elijah and his God revive our spirits," he chanted.

Falsehoods

Traveling through the brush we stumbled upon what we believed was an ancient relic or a place used for sacrificial burnings. It appeared to be a large oven—a monolith that seemed both finished and unfinished at the same time. Even the tools to shape them where there, as if the workmen had to flee suddenly.

We should have just kept moving, but some of the men felt there might be clues and warnings on the monolith. Another man and I grabbed some of the tools, which apparently were made by skilled Assyrian craftsmen. We discussed one of the stories about them, which concerned the Assyrian ransacking of Hamath and the Shalmaneser victory. But in the middle of our conversation, U said they were lies—that Hamath had been victorious against the Assyrians. U mentioned how the Assyrians used false information, how they planted seeds of exaggeration to confuse potential enemies.

Most on the trail were unable to read, so many did not know the details, but parts of the monolith did contain figures with detailed executions. As U explained the inscription about Hamath to the men, many of them laughed, though most became more emboldened. It was a glimpse into the enemy's strategic game, and it boosted morale.

The Gauntlet

After U, Al Biqa and I escaped the slaughter on the Orontes River, we managed to find a fortified commercial road from Damascus, a passageway with protected villages. Those villages were Barga, Argana and Adennu, also known as Ada. The partial victory of King Irhuleni of Hamath in Qarqar secured some of those villages, which gave us a slim possibility of passage home. The road between Damascus and Biqa was our only hope for survival, but our challenges were far from over. Al Biqa had a leg injury, and U was numb from the battle. There was a kind of uncomfortable emptiness about this road. The Assyrian bloodshed had most people hiding. We were covered in its dry, cracking clay, we had lost weight and strength. Straddling in the hot setting sun, the three of us were in dire need of comfort—emotional and beyond.

"Should we go back?" questioned U.

"Back to what? asked Al Biqa.

"Back to death," I commented in a near whisper.

"How can we live when all has perished?" Al Biqa said.

"We need to live. We fought and held back the raid," I asserted.

In a voice so utterly dry due to a lack of water, Al Biqa said:

"We have no army. There are piles of bodies in the river."

I reminded them all that we represented a king and that going home would give our people hope. To which Al Biqa replied that he wondered not only where our comrades were, but where were our kings.

"I come from Zarephath," I explained, "ruled by a selfish king, King Ahab, but I know our comrades' lives and deaths will not be in vain. We will find water. This land is rich. This is why Shalmeneser wants it so desperately."

I was asked if I still had faith in defeat.

"Show some respect Al Biqa," urged U.

The Boy from Zarephath

Al Biqa hopped over to a stone wall and sat upon it to rest. "Let us camp here, men," he said. "I am tired."

So we all fall asleep, practically leaning upon each other. The next morning I began to remove bark from a tree limb, starring at Al Biqa as I did so, trying to estimate Al Biqa's height. U slowly opened his eyes as a large caterpillar crawled along the bridge of his nose. He grabbed it and swallowed it whole.

"What are you doing, Jonah?" Al Biqa asked.

"Making you a walking cane. But we have to get fresh water to clean your injury."

"And to cleanse our skin."

"Yes."

We gathered ourselves together and continued our journey. Soon, in the distance, the village of Barga was in our site. Just a year before, I recalled, the cities en route were torched by Shalmaneser. My comrades and I fell into confusion. The road was a more direct passage home, but one laden with spies, desperate clans, and limited resources. Then, suddenly, a whisper came from the roadside brush:

"Men, are you scorpion or butterflies?"

"Whose asking? We are both," said Al Biqa.

The whisper continued: "Your very lives depend on the right answer."

With our tired eyes we tried to search the brush, but as we took a few steps closer to the road's edge, spears began to poke through, which prevented us from getting any closer.

"If you want our demise, then we are scorpions," said U.

"Let's go, Jonah," Al Biqa insisted.

"Did you fight with the kings?" came a female whisper.

"I for Que," said Jonah.

"I for Damascus," followed Al Biqa.

"I for Que" concluded U.

Four women came out of the brush with ropes and ushered us into a deep pit within the leaves and vines which had shredded fabric strung across for concealment. Inside this tent-like pit was a women carrying a baby. Three other young women were digging into the earth, looking for water. Hanging on ropes were sacks of water dripping into vessels that seemed designed to filter out impurities. The women started to wash our bodies and feed us bread and berries from the brush. It was a miracle. All of life's necessities in this one tent pit. We were stripped naked and given the garments of our enemies.

"Sleep tonight and go tomorrow. You will die if you do not wear this. Spies are searching," said one of the women—the one who seemed to make all of the decisions for the entire group.

We were unable to sleep, mostly because these women were so beautiful. Soon, however, U and Al

Biqa did fall asleep, and I remained awake to listen to the women tell of the raids and the strategic patterns of the Assyrian armies.

"Why did you help us?" I asked.

"Because you are the only one men we have seen for six months," the leader of the women replied.

"Six months and no men?"

"Yes. The only men around are the Assyrians, but for two days we have not seen them. Have you defeated them?"

"No, we have not. Why don't you come with us?"

"No," she said, "we will stay here and wait for more men like you." She paused. "Who is your God?"

"YHWH."

"The god of the false prophets?"

I looked deep into her eyes. "I truly believe that YHWH has positioned me for safe passage," I said in as strong and calm a voice as possible.

The young women put her hand on my face and said, "I believe you."

She told me to avoid Ada as it was a trap, and to share that news with the other men when they awoke. "The word is that anyone who travels past Argana never comes back. I asked how she knew so much, and she said that many Assyrians have all but confessed right there in the pit.

The Boy from Zarephath

Al Biqa, U and I departed at sunset and headed west, loaded with supplies—and hope.

U and Al Biqa

As I got to know the men, I seemed to have discovered more about U than about Al Biqa. On the surface U was rough and unhappy. I suspected he was that way even before the destruction of his village and the battle at Qarqar. While on this trek home he was inclined to start quarrels. Perhaps his injured ego, it was almost understandable.

"We are cowards," said Al Biqa at one point.

"We are weak," U retorted.

"We left our comrades," admitted Al Biqa with his head between his legs. "I have done bad things in my youth."

"We all have."

"No, I thought I was more important than my mentors, even my ancestors."

"We are not going to make it home."

"We made it this far," I said, "and we are not alone. Others will come and strengthen us." "As a young boy I was always a stranger, and I assumed many different identities to try to stay safe and free. My family drifted from Asia to Egypt. It was survival, but it taught me one thing: never love something or anything too much."

"Then I see your heart is just fine," smirked U. "It is empty, with plenty of room to be filled."

"You love life," I said. "You mustered the courage to fight. Neither of us are cowards. When we enlisted for a battle, we understood it could be our last."

"I am a stranger, but my home is Egypt. As a young men I made many enemies," Al Biqa grumbled.

I asked him how.

"It was because of my hatred for those who practice magic," he explained. "I challenged people—scholars, even—in the streets, like a madman."

U asked why he did that.

"My father lost all his money to them and spent five years in prison."

"Where is your father now?" I asked.

"He is sick. We all have sick fathers. But do not feel sorry for him, for he is one hundred twenty years old."

"Where is he?"

"In Cairo."

"We all have made mistakes," I said. "But we can learn from those who made them first."

The nights were dark, and the glow of war was still faintly perceptible from behind us. We seldom looked back. We laid down and looked up at the sky that glowed with hope. To us, the pattern of the stars resembled a path home. But what in reality was in front of us was a path we were unable to see. In the wilderness we knew we would have to contend both with the swift hand of fate's judgment and the insects that bit us and made us their dinner.

U and Al Biqa slept as I kept watch with my head perched upon a rock. The constant chill stiffened my body and aged my face. I was in desperate need of some natural medicinal oils to replenish my pores and calm my beating heart. I closed my eyes for a moment and thought about my brother. Even though I was fifteen years older than him, we had a bond and our hearts beat as one. Knowing he was worried about me made me more determined to make it home. At that point, Elijah entered my mind in a memory.

"Look Jonah, come to the window" he said, pointing to the heavens. "What do you see?"

"Large and small stars" I replied. I was ten-years-old in this recollection.

"What do they tell you?" Elijah asked.

"I do not know."

"Tomorrow the stars will be at your window. And they will be there every day, Jonah."   I returned from the memory and saw Barga is in the distance, but she did not look safe.

"Jonah, we have to get away. It is not safe," said U.

As we walked off the dusty trail, two men on horseback spotted us. We quickly grabbed Al Biqa, supported him with one arm each, and hid in a cave. The cave was wider and deeper than any other I had seen, and as we stumbled to the floor we heard the horses fall. We took a peek out of the cave opening and saw the two men as they shouted at their horses to get up. They were yanking at the bridles, but the animals would not move. "Just leave them there," one man barked to the other.

The two of them entered the cave, stomping on the muddy clay and calling out for us. "Cowards!" one yelled. "We will not harm you!" shouted the other. They repeated these phrases as they got closer. Outside, their horses began to whinny in strange tones. With every step the men took toward us, the horses grew more flustered.

"What is wrong with those beasts?"

The men may have been hungry for blood, but they retreated because they feared the horses might leave them stranded. They called off their search, got back on their beasts of burden, and rode away in silence.

"It was the smell of swine on you, Al Biqa, that scared them away," U smirked, "and the sweat on Jonah's forehead that brought them here in the first place."

Once we left the coolness of the cave, Al Biqa's leg seemed to improve. But at the same time, he grew more silent. Perhaps it was his age (he was older than the two of us). Plus, he had lost everything. U and I still had hope of seeing our families; Al Biqa lived only with the hope of returning to Egypt to live out his last days with the memories of his ancestors.

Avoid

We had to stomp through challenging terrain to avoid stepping on fragments of humanity left behind by the Assyrian armies. We gathered leather and soft bark, which we were able to wrap around our ankles to protect them from thorny, rocky, splintered brush. Al Biqa no longer needed our aid because something happened in the cave that gave him—all three of us, in fact—additional strength and hope. The bloodthirsty men were not too far away; their dust trail seemed to be a distant lantern in the gentle breeze.

As night fell, our thirst became nearly intolerable. We knew that villages near rivers were too dangerous, and as we wandered away, our chances for clean water became more desperate.

What with the effects of war and all that follows, we felt fortunate to be alive—but every step into the unknown wilderness made survival that much harder. It was a landscape untamed by development, surrounded by burned crops, populated by hollow, unforgiving homes. We were like animals, those that scamper on the ground and fly in the air—afraid of mankind. Even when we would offer bread to trap a bird, the suspicious bird would not take it from us. The animals had changed. God was more silent than ever.

What we needed was rain.

As we followed the stars west, an odor of dead fish made us trek to what we assumed would be a foul patch of water. Moments later we walked into a dry bed and saw only tiny carcasses and discarded nets— no water. It had once been a thriving lake, ripe with living things, and we were miserably disheartened to see what we now saw. We decide to sit on a plank of petrified timber, which resembled an old fisherman's skiff.

The silence was broken by our growling stomachs, but we were modestly comforted by a full moon and the steady cool breeze. As U and Al Biqa drifted into their dreams and nightmares, I remained awake, angered by life. Why, I asked myself, was the world the way it was? Even Elijah was homeless and had to scrounge for sustenance. But he had saved us once, and after my mother, I considered him my greatest mentor. He had it hard, but considered his hardships blessings. Whenever Elijah spoke, it was like a benevolent lion, powerful but gentle. His words were words I will never forget.

The Boy from Zarephath

As I lay on the hard timber I remembered Elijah's words. I could hear him speak as if I were in my bedroom and he was elsewhere in the house:

"Chava, tell me why you trusted my promises, promises made by God. After all, I was a stranger."

"The night before I met you," mother said, "I was up on the roof. Never before had I risked being up there, but this night I did. I saw Ahab's palace and smelled the incense that drifted into the village. The aroma was hollow, and gave no hope. I reclined and looked to the stars. I closed my eyes. I asked aloud if my son will be a good man. Before the drought and famine, there were many good men. But all that has changed, and that's why I need to know."

"Jonah will be a good man," Elijah assured her.

In my bedroom, I sat up on my bed to give my full attention to the conversation I was overhearing.

"But it was the God that brought me here to you," Elijah said. "What other validation is there? God knows what is in your heart more than you do."

"Elijah," mother whispered, "at times I have a guilty feeling of past sins. I have a boy without a father."

I sank back down into the covers. I did not understand what mother meant, but I felt sorrow in her tone. I stared at the ceiling (much as I stared at the stars while letting this memory take over me). The challenges back then were momentous, and the challenges as I sat on the hard timber were just as substantial. My protector as a boy was both mother and YHWH; now it was solely God.

Elijah continued in my memory:

"Many times we exaggerate our guilt, and a conscience is a testimony to the quality of women you are."

I sensed it was a wonderful thing that Elijah had said to mother. I leaped out of bed and took a peek out of the door. They did not notice I was watching them. Mother was sitting by the stove, across from Elijah. The joy on her face eliminated all my stress. Whenever I thought about the words from Elijah, renewed strength was always the result.

With U and Al Biqa sleeping beside me, I knew I must hold on to those memories to make sure we all reached our homes once again.

Climbing the Wall

We drifted back onto the road and encountered another city covered with blood and sand. In just a few months the desert had reclaimed it. There was enough sand to reach to the top of the city walls.

The Boy from Zarephath

Al Biqa ran up a slope. I tried to stop him because a breeze of burning incense came my way—but it was too late. Arrows narrowly missed his head. He stumbled down the back edge of sand. We heard a thunderous rubbing of metal. Thirty men stormed over the wall. Al Biqa, U and I huddled together. I assumed the men were from Ada, a large city that no doubt ran out of food, forcing its men to form a gang that violently sought out the nearest resources. Thirty men faced us in a long arc, forbidding us to escape. U stomped his feet on the ground.

"Come get us, you fools, you thirsty fools," he yelled.

Al Biqa and I looked at each other. We didn't know what to do. One of the men in the group looked at Al Biqa and said he knew him.

"You are a trickster who plays with the scales," he said. He was missing a leg. He walked closer to Al Biqa. "Speak up, deceiver."

U started to stomp the ground even harder.

"Stop screaming," the one-legged man said. "No one can hear you."

U pounded his chest and moved his body like a duck. Some of the men laughed, but drew their bows nonetheless. Suddenly, the earth started to sink under him, like the trickling sand of an hourglass. Below him was a bone-dry well covered at the top with planks. We moved closer to U, and the three of us leaped in.

The men shouted: "Kill them, kill them, they are sick, they are sick...!" The one-legged man fell on us, which added to our combined weight and broke the planks that covered the well. Once the earth gave way, the four of us cascaded into well, more than thirty feet below. The impact at the bottom was softened by a layer grass and bare, pliable branches. The man with one leg ended up buried beneath us. We heard the men on the surface yelling, calling out to their comrade. The three of us stood up and embraced each other. The men above started to kick sand on top of us; they seemed to have instantly given up on their comrade.

The violent fall had disturbed a portion of the well wall, and at our feet trickled water through a small portal. As the men above continued to yell and kick sand down upon us, darkness encompassed the well, which was now more like a cell of doom. The water rose past our ankles. It appeared to be highly pressurized, as if it had been locked away since before the walled city was built. It reached our waists in seconds. The water was sweet, and for a moment it was thirst and not drowning that consumed my mind. Deadly thirst can make anyone insane.

We treaded water as we floating upward to our enemies. On U's and Al Biqa's faces were nothing but anger and rage; they were ready to defend themselves—and each other. Half a minute later, the rising torrent ejected us out of the well, higher even than the walls of the city. The sloping sand dunes softened our fall. The geyser created a flow of water that acted as our escape route.

In a short time we found ourselves on the shore of a river. A good night's sleep helped us forget the way the day had started.

On the beach, the soothing current flowing southward continued to give us hope. When I was a teenager, the true meaning of hope was more a mental than a physical thing. It was inexorably linked to the time when mother first showed me how to pray.

"My son," I remember her saying to me, "sit here." She pointed to a spot beside her. "Jonah, we must gather these thoughts of hope deep in our hearts and release them, from our bellies to our hearts and into the voices in our mind."

"What do you mean?" I asked.

"The more you release your secret thoughts to God, the more attention you will receive."

"I do not understand."

"Well, we have hope when life is hard, but we must remain hopeful when life is good."

We closed our eyes, and mother said a prayer out loud, thanking God for my health. I learned that day that we need to communicate with God, not only when life is in peril but when life shines blessings upon us. "Speaking quietly to God," mother smiled, "keeps the heart from letting deceitfulness creep in."

The Boy from Zarephath

I had seen much deceitfulness, much treachery, as a young boy. I have also seem much love and hope—particularly the love and hope of mothers and fathers. Certainly without good mothers and fathers, men like U and Al Biqa would not even exist.

The Hinder Sea

Deuteronomy 11:24 says: "Every place whereon the soul of your foot shall tread shall be yours: from the wilderness, and Lebanon, from the river, the river Euphrates, even unto the hinder sea shall be your border."

We were fifty miles from Qarqar, not far from the sea, and scorched by the stinging sun. As we trekked southward, we were in need of horses, or a boat, but all we were able to find was abandoned and shuttered docks, barren villages, and a few small bands of confused, helpless people. Many others had joined the armies or fled their homes. Whenever we saw a well in the distance, one of us would run ahead to check it out—but most of the time it was full of sand. We dug for insects and even ate some grass. The sea was harsh and the fish had disappeared from the shores of the Mediterranean Sea. The earth seemed cursed. I remembered stories mother told me of when my father brought home a harvest of sardines. He had been working on the sea and was proud of his design work on the boats. His journey for employment took him away from us for weeks. Mother explained how he had persevered the sardines for the long trip back home, which involved brining them in water, putting them in a clay vessel, and burying them underground. She used this method when food became scarce during the drought. The little she had from our garden was pickled and stored in the earth. Soon, however, the drought exhausted all our resources, regardless of how well we tried to avoid that.

When I walked through this now barren land, I glanced at the field where I was certain there must be buried vessels of salted sardines or cured fruits. When we passed the dry villages, rodent-like holes covered the landscape. Crashing waves washed the sins away of this cursed region, and the salt burned away the tears of its inhabitants. Al Biqa suddenly yelled out:

"There's a skiff coming in!"

I saw it, too, as did U, and the three of us ran down the rocky slope. It was a blue skiff, with casting nets and two oars. We cried with happiness and threw our arms around each other. I was eager to cast those nets and push back into the sea. The skiff was almost twenty feet long, room enough for five men and stable enough to haul a mighty catch. We paddled into the rough sea and tied down the net to the side. Al Biqa controlled the vessel while U and I tossed the net. Then we stood and waited. Within a minute, the net tugged and jolted the skiff. We pulled the net onto the boat. The weight of the fish exceeded our own combined weight; twenty sardines, many weighing as much as five pounds, flapped into the skiff. Al Biqa started to turn us back toward shore. As we separated the sardines we saw a baby octopus stretch out its tentacles. Al Biqa took an oar and positioned it over the octopus, but the animal wrapped its tentacles around the oar.

"This beautiful sea creature belongs to God," Al Biqa said—and he put the octopus back into the sea.

We had used all our strength paddling into the sea, lifting our bounty, and paddling back, and I almost passed out after we reached the shore. But I remained conscious enough to watch U start to tear the fish apart, as Al Biqa gathered up some straw and twigs to clean the catch.

The next morning we decided to make our way home by the blue skiff, which blended in with the sea. Only a glimmer from the sun would alert our enemies to our presence. We took our chances. We were energized. The sea and the sun temporarily evaporated all our memories so that we could concentrate on paddling. We took turns with the oars. We covered each other with sand-soaked linens that we had salvaged on the beach. As we coasted along the sea on southern currents, we grew excited by the possibilities that lay ahead. Then, as U and I worked the oars and as Al Biqa sat on the bow, Al Biqa shouted:

"Watch out!"

We ducked down low to hide ourselves from a warship that poke up on the horizon. The ship was probably a scout looking for deserters or for the Assyrian army. Or perhaps it was a vessel taken over by refugees. We kept calm and crouched as low as possible on the skiff, trying against all odds to paddle to a nearby cove.

The day was spent scouting out the cove, which was once was a fishing port and served as a protection for smaller vessels in the stormy season. All was deserted now, resources taken, not even a hidden morsel of food or a scurrying rodent had survived the war. There was only fear and death. Not even any bodies or the smell of death remained—just emptiness mixed with sadness. We came to a tall bench, which we assumed had been part of pub where wine was served and customers were jolly.

Al Biqa tugged at me and suggested we leave immediately.

The sun was shining. There was a cool breeze. U ran up a heap of trash to get a better look at the ocean.

"I can see past this inlet," he announced. "No warships. We should go."

We were hungry and had little strength to paddle, but U was correct: leaving the cove was the best advice. The men with the bows and spears were too far away to reach us. But we hastened our pace on the skiff anyway, knowing that the clan of marauders could still track our route. Before long we were so weak from lack of food and water that we could hardly even think. We pushed ourselves south until the sun begun to set. Under the cover of darkness, we found a beach. On it were children.

Day 3

When one hears children laughing, it is a sign that peace and security dwell nearby.

The children spotted us as our skiff cast long shadows onto the beach. Al Biqa, U and I dropped our nets into the sea as we approached the beach, under the assumption that we might still gather some fish. And we did, in fact, gather a small school, which we offered to a fishing tribe we found waiting in the near distance, beyond where the children played on the shore. .

That night was clear. The children continued to frolic, the men removed the scales from the fish, and then the women cleaned marrow from the bones. The tribe leader had deep wrinkles that crossed over his left eye and shot across his nose down to his cheek. He was pale from many years of staying inside; his skin was allergic to the sun. He turned to me and said:

"Are you young men willing to trade your skiff for food, friendship and safety, now and forever?"

"No" I said. "We appreciate your hospitality, but we have families who rely on us. Abandoning them is not an option." I looked toward Al Biqa and U for confirmation, and they nodded affirmatively.

A women came over, kissed me and touched my hand.

"I need you," she whispered.

U and Al Biqa went back to the skiff, knowing that our sole means of transportation could be stolen if we weren't careful.

Meanwhile, the women's touch made me wonder if it were a sincere sign of affection, or a desperate plea for help. U and Al Biqa were already in the skiff. I could see in their expressions that they were calling me to come. Before I let go of the women's hand, I asked her name.

"Ruth," she replied

"What a beautiful name."

Day 4

It was a day of memories, precipitated by a storm we encountered in our little skiff. Not unsurprisingly, I had many memories of storms—storms that brought death, storms that were more ruthless than the armies of Assyria, storms from which no one can escape, storms with no warnings. It seemed to happen many times when I was a boy. They would give me terrible headaches. Mother would cradle me in her arms and put warm towels on my head until I could fall asleep. She tried changing my diet to alleviate the aches. Whenever she could afford it, she asked the town doctor to visit, but he could never provide an answer.

One day when I awoke, Elijah's soft touch made my soul seemed reborn. That's when I came to believe, and that's when the headaches stopped.

As U, Biqa and I struggled to keep the skiff from overturning, I stared into the storm clouds, which seemed to want to mete out more punishment. We were determined not to let the storm devour us. Then a mighty wave with fangs of foam hovered over our heads. Simultaneously, U and Al Biqa yelled "YHWH!"

My friends knew nothing of this God, but their shout turned the dark sea to an instant calm. The three of us, wet and exhausted, gripped the rim of the skiff, stood up and cried out in joy. We embraced and looked to the heavens, where the sun started to glow. One hundred meters away there was a small island, and we paddled in its direction. Despite the calm and the sun, there was a large, monstrous fish flapping on the beach. We disembarked and huddled under a cluster of palm trees as the thunderous sea creature snapped tree limbs. In our malnourished state we laughed—though it was an agonizing laugh.

Before too long, we were able to gather up enough fish to have one of the best meals we had had in quite some time, Still, we knew we had to get off the island within a day or two before the dead carcasses brought flies and foul odor.

Day 5

As we continued our journey, Al Biqa kept much of his past a secret. But as our friendship grew, he revealed why he came to fight in the war at Qarqar. He had a brief romance weeks before enlisting with the Egyptian armies. Always feeling like an outsider because of his past transgressions as a swindler, he met a women who had many children. She hailed from nobility. He loved her—and not just because she was willing to pardon those past transgressions.

Getting to know Al Biqa left no confusion as to his real heart. He told us the woman's nobility was in peril when her first husband and brother traded goods with enemies on the western borders of Egypt. Losing her nobility to a commoner might protect her from harsh judgment. But on their wedding day, her father, brother and the brother's wife were imprisoned far away. Al Biqa's disappointment led him to the Orontes River, which is where I found an eternal friend.

Day 6

In the chaos of the storm we were swept up north to Byblos, which had once been a great city. Al Biqa knew the history of Byblos because of its historic trade with Egypt. A shallow grave of great ships marked our arrival. Suddenly, we heard the whistling of spears raining on us. We plunged into the sea using the skiff as a shield, treading with our feet. We managed to get far enough away from the reach of the spears. Beneath our feet we felt the cold current pushing our bodies south. We clung to the skiff like an underwater sail. We saw some men on the rotting marooned ships. Some stood up, but all they could do was take notice of our swift departure.

Soon we were far away, but trembling from the icy currents below. With U's assistance, I helped Al Biqa aboard, then we headed southward at top speed, and finally came to a beach that was covered with roaming sand cats. We tried not to be overly concerned—even though sand cats are not known to be so close to the sea.

"Let's get out of here, Jonah," Al Biqa said, shaking.

"I'm worried about Al Biqa," U said. "We need to get to shelter."

"Yes," I agreed. "But I sense danger, U. All those sand cats are here because they must have fled a fire or approaching armies."

U and Al Biqa looked at me.

"Let's listen to Jonah," U acknowledged, glancing at Al Biqa. "Hopefully the wind will die down. Let's stay put for a little while."

Al Biqa concurred, realizing that the armies could be over five miles wide and rapidly on their way toward the beach.

"What do we do, Jonah?" U asked,

"I still think we must ride it out. Stay. And keep Al Biqa as warm as we can. Let's cover him with the fishing nets. They're not ideal for warmth, but every little bit will help."

As the night began to set, the breezes settled down.

Day 7

The salt of the sea and the morning dew soaked into our bones. Each of us dreamt of something hot to drink and of sweet dates to eat. Al Biqa lifted his head from the net.

"Look!" Al Biqa called out. "Wild date trees."

We turned to the rocky edge of the beach where the wind battled the trees, which made their palms wave like hands greeting visitors. We hadn't seen that before. We hurried over. The area seemed untouched because of the rocky mountains behind them. They formed a natural barrier that defended the beautiful beach. Birds feasting on falling dates were the our only companions—and we scared them away when we took over their job Al Biqa dug his hands and feet into the hot sand to thaw his frail body. We were energized by the sweet sugary fruit. We laughed. It was the first time in days. We felt secure. We had our very first uninterrupted sleep. Home felt near.

Day 8

I knew that when we finally reached Zarephath it would be the last time I would see Al Biqa and U. I recalled when Elijah left us in the wilderness. His sole security was YHWH. Mother and I wept when he left. Elijah told me I was the first of mankind to wake from eternal sleep. He told how God looked into my heart, and that my heart brought peace to Him. I was too young to understand the meaning of a peaceable heart, but sitting on the beach with U and Al Biqa, I believed my two comrades were no different. They, too, had peaceable hearts.

The Boy from Zarephath

Day 9

Fog excited us. It appeared like a secret veil that cloaks the innocence of a beautiful women. The sea had tired us. We had enough food, which we had picked up along the way. Al Biqa felt that we should stay away from the shore just a little while longer. As we paddled around a bend, the sea became choppy. Sea creatures feasted and birds gathered overhead. A seaside village appeared ahead and gave us hope that the raging war was far from these parts. Al Biqa sat up, took the oar from U, and started to paddle away from it.

"What are you doing Al Biqa?" I asked.

"We are still not safe enough to be distracted by the village."

I put my hand on his back. "I think you need to rest, my friend. Why shouldn't we make port?"

"I just want to get home," he whispered hoarsely. "No more running and hiding."

"Yes, I understand. But we need rest. And look closely at the village. Shutters are open, roads are clear, roofs are undamaged."

The two men thought about it.

The sky began to darken and a chill swept in. The village on the beach looked beautiful—and abandoned. A fleet of ships appeared on our stern as if placed there by the dark clouds.

"Jonah, behind us!" cried out Al Biqa.

It was a menacing galley vessel he saw—and then we all saw—with dark red sails. It overshadowed three vessels behind it. The four ships varied in size and speed. The largest one lowered a skiff from its port side, with seven or eight men in it. They seemed unusually taller than most men. Al Biqa told me to hurry. He and U also asked me if I were seeing what they saw. I said I did.

"Should we trust them?" Al Biqa asked.

"They haven't killed us yet," I replied.

We pounded the sea with our skiff, creating a foam streak that followed us straight into a dark, rocky cave. Inside the cave was a great army. Arrows were ready to strike them—and strike them they did. The army released a thousand arrows to the fleet from the darkness of the cave. The general timed his attack before the tide would fill the cave. The rest of the army, hidden in the village, climbed the roofs and sent fiery arrows that penetrated the port sides of the turning ships. The beach, once peaceful and barren, now had constant thunderous cries of men, who frantically reloaded their bows and finished the brutish attack on the men who had once been on course to finish us off.

The battle was short, but terrifying. Al Biqa, U and I leapt into the arms of the victorious men, even though we did not know their origins. We soon came to realize they were a part of the Egyptian squad returning from the war of Qarqar. They were the wall that kept the Assyrians and other unknown northern forces from making their way south. Few of them spoke; they merely grunted and nodded. We rested on the crowded beach with them—about six hundred strong. The shore was bountiful with enough sea life to sustain a large army.

U, Al Biqa and I rested on a hill, away from the bloodshed. From that view the northern army's vessels illuminated the night horizon as they drifted on the sea into a reflecting sliver of the setting sun. Like torches that light a sacrifice to ask God for forgiveness, we asked God to forgive us for being part of man's rage against one another.

Day 10

In the morning we searched for our skiff, running up and down the beach in search of it. Apparently it had drifted away or was taken or destroyed by the Egyptian army. Al Biqa was very tired and I feared he would not make it. His frail body would be unable to handle any more walking, or any more war. U and I pondered what we should do. A group of men approached us and asked about Al Biqa's garments, on which there were markings related to Egyptian royalty.

"Have you taken your garments from a royal?" asked one of the men.

"My friend is no thief," U shouted angrily.

"Take it easy, my friend. Didn't we just save you?"

A short, muscular man asked to look at Al Biqa and came closer, but U interceded and asked if the man was a doctor. I sensed something in the man that made believe he did indeed have medical knowledge, so I helped part the way so that he could look Al Biqa.

"This man is dehydrated," the man said after a looking him over. "My comrades are now gathering water from a crack in the mountain. If they hurry, we can save your friend." He turned back to Al Biqa and asked for his name. Al Biqa whispered it, and then the doctor pronounced to his comrades:

"This man is royalty. Run to the others and tell them to hurry. We need water for a son of royalty. His name is Al Biqa."

It was U, instead of the doctor's comrades, who ran off to tell the others. Water is always a life-giver. So many stories of its power... and as I thought about those stories I saw U in the distance carrying a heavy cistern. When he arrived with it, U dusted off a large shell and gave Al Biqa a drink of the sweet water. I rubbed some of it on his forehead and into his hair to cool him down. I held one of his hands, U held the other. Our compassionate actions let the others know there we truly and deeply cared for this man, and that compelled some of the others, who were busy devouring figs, to come over and offer us some of the fruit. "Eat these," one of them said. "The sweetness will spark the soul."

Al Biqa smiled. As a boy I had heard of stories of many Egyptians who had not an iota of kindness inside of them—but today the Egyptians showed us a compassionate side we would never forget.

Day 11

In the evening, the tide came in, the moon was a full circle, and despite the fact that our skiff was covered in arrows, we had hope that it was in good enough shape to take us home. The men told us that the sea and shores to Zarephath were protected by Hamath, who were able to push back the enemy in Qarqar. They lost three-thousand, but in the process they took down triple that number from the armies of Shalmaneser.

Day 12

As a stiff morning fog rolled in, our bodies were equally stiff from sleeping in unconformable positions. An Egyptian soldier looked at us and asked how many days we had been at sea. Al Biqa told him eleven days, and the man said it was just a seven day journey on a skiff or three days on a war vessel. Al Biqa stood up and stared into the man's eyes sternly and said:

"We are not men of war trained in the art of strategic warfare, but we understand its place in the world. In the face of evil we became friends. We are a testimony that men like you are willing to preserve the life of children, good men and women. It is not the length of the journey that's important, but the ones with whom you take that journey."

One soldier kneeled down and said, "You are great men."

We gathered ourselves and pushed into the sea. The sun was gentle and the currents were our chariot guides. We looked back at the men on shore. One shouted. "Pass the twin sentinel perched in the sea, and a legion of Egyptians will take your friend home."

I stood up and saluted.

"Victory awaits," they called out. "Victory awaits."

The Legion

After a half day's journey we reached the two sentinels, where a dozen vessels were going into port.

Al Biqa asked if were going to stop again, and I said yes, that we needed to get better care for you.

"A legion of Egyptians may get you home faster than we can," I insisted. "Going to Cairo is too dangerous to travel without protection, my friend."

"We will never see each other again."

"We will write to one another."

As U steered us into port we saw a thin man with branding markings on his left shoulder. It spelled out Huriya, which Al Biqa told us means "Freedom." The man helped us onto the platform as we tied up our boat. We walked to a camp where many people were preparing for battle and making a feast to feed the army. The thin man never looked at me but talked only to U and Al Biqa. I wasn't sure why. Some prejudice, perhaps.

We arrived at a place where a group gathered that was heading back to Cairo. There were dozens of wounded men. We talked with them about Al Biqa's condition. They assured us he would be fine. As night fell, we found a good place to sleep. The thin man said his name was Horus, and he finally broke his silence against me.

"You are Jonah from Zarephath," he stated.

"Yes," I acknowledged. "Do I know you?"

"You made it through the famine. How?" There was a hint of jealousy and anger in his voice. "You lived through the drought, as I did. I remember the old man that everyone wanted to kill. He lived with you."

"How do you know so much? I assume you are the same age as I."

"I remember the whispers," he said. "How did you and your mother survive? My own mother would tell of the resilient glow on your mother's face in the mist of all the peril."

"I don't remember any Egyptian boys, then."

"Zarephath, as you know, was full of drifters. We stayed for a moon and then returned to Cairo. My mother would call us to the window when your mother walked about. We stayed in a three-story house that overlooked the city."

As the man spoke with me, U make arrangements to have Al Biqa join the caravan to Egypt. Horus and I continued to question one another, but I gathered that his mind was sick and weak, and his angry, jealous digging into the past showed how madness often follows war.

"My friend," he said suddenly, "I have to say goodbye."

Horus turned away and stared at the sea. There were many unanswered questions about his mother's curiosity.

We met with the caravan that promised to take Al Biqa home. He was still weak, but his eyes smiled strongly and tears came to his eyes as we touched each other's hands and brought our foreheads close.

"You are the bother I never had, Jonah. And U, your vigor reassures me eager to finish our journey. I will miss you both."

A great caravan of broken men trekked into the sunset. U and I accompanied them for two days.

Reveal

My frail friend, broken by our perilous journey, took a deep breath as familiar faces on the road to his home smiled at him and greeted him as a lost relative newly found. We had seen no children once in our trek westward, which tested our faith in YHWH, but as the children gathered around us toward our journey's end, it gave us much needed comfort. Finally we felt safe.

Some people approached us and asked if the Assyrian armies were behind us. I told them no, and that to our knowledge some of the Kings had lost their confidence.

When I saw U's home I become more homesick myself. Seeing him make it this far, surrounded by love, made me more anxious to see my mother and brother. As we pushed open a great cedar door, U's father lay there on a bare bed, stiff, worn and thin with age and worry, surrounded by his other children. Both of U's sisters fell to his feet and wept. His brother, a year younger than him, greeted us in tears. The world was at war and we were the survivors. U's father sat up, turned to us and exhaled:

"My first born is home."

U felt a jolt of vigor when he heard these words from his father.

"Of all my children, you have your mother's eyes and her spirit of adventure."

U lowered his head, and it was clear he was apologizing for having left in the first place. "I know, U," his father uttered, knowing what his son wanted to say. "Many men perish, but you halted the Assyrian Empire. You and your friend put a marvelous and necessary dent in history."

"How do you know such things, my father? The war continues, and our city is mostly inhabited by women. If the men survived they would be here by now. I regret to say this, father, but many are in the spirit realm."

"Look around you. Your sisters and brother play and sing, there is food and drink, the sweat on your forehead was not wasted. Your journey home will never be forgotten."

"Father," U said, "I have no children to continue your seed. I caused your heart to bleed in worry."

The Boy from Zarephath

"No my son. You are my first born, and a first born always has it hard. We are all learning. We had it hard, and because of those hardships you were made strong."

The father touched U's overgrown beard and told him that the village and their family always sent along prayers to him. "I knew you were alive," he said. "You possess your mother's strength and determination."

"Oh, father..."

U put his head on his father's shoulder and wept.

Then his father asked about me and Al Biqa. U told him that I was Jonah from Zarephath—and his father asked me to step closer because he wanted to look in my eyes. "There is something in them that brings memories," he said.

"They are hungry, they are hungry" shouted his sisters.

Suddenly, the sisters began to sing a song that was at once joyful and sad, and while they sang they began to prepare food. I reclined into a sack of wool and fell asleep. Al Biqa was in dire need of rest, as well, and reclined into another sack of wool. Both of us were overwhelmed by the compassion of U's household.

When I awoke, U's father was staring at me.

The Boy from Zarephath

"You are the boy from Zarephath," he cried out—not as a question, but a statement of fact. "Jonah, yes? Well, Jonah, come over to me if you have the strength."

U's sisters were now helping Al Biqa and me clean our hands for dinner, using linen from a hot basin. Their affectionate help hindered my ability to abide by their father's request. Still, I tried, and finally made my way over to him.

"U told me of your days in Zarephath, during the time of drought and famine," he said.

"Did he tell you about a miracle I witnessed?" I asked.

"Yes."

U's father sat up from his bed, touched my forehead, stared into my eyes, and finally gently stated: "This is the boy, my children. This is the boy."

His daughters stopped singing and asked what he meant.

"This is the miracle from Zarephath, my children. Thirteen years ago, Jonah was ten. I was in Zarephath, and witnessed Jonah brought back to life. Jonah is now twenty three. God protected my son and has now blessed our home. I once laughed at the prophets and did not believe in God."

"Are you the one," Al Biqa asked, "the one U once told us about?"

The Boy from Zarephath

"Are you the boy the prophet raised from the dead?" asked U.

I looked from one to the other:

"I am."

One of U's sister insisted that we get some more rest, and that the questions should cease for a while.

"But I'd like to tell my story," I insisted. "I am weak and tired of running, and the story of my life needs to be told."

The room was silent. All ears were on me.

"My second chance at life did not begin with what your father witnessed," I began. "It started six months before then. As you know, the land governed by Ahab experienced a drought of almost four years." One of the sisters nodded; she remembered well. "I recall the cold silence as a boy. I was ten. Everything around us was dying. Mother hid the reality of the times from me, but years later she told of how the prophet Elijah came to stay with us. She was walking home from the market. Such a trip usually brought only heartache. That day the only food she was able to purchase was bread and oil. A stranger to Zarephath, who had traveled for over a hundred miles, sought out my mother and found her in a most desperate state. Elijah was his name. He sensed my mother possessed a good heart. I believe that each felt pity for the other."

The Boy from Zarephath

As I continued to tell my story, other people started to enter U's home and it became a citadel of curiosity. I was reminded of Kings 17:8-16 and recited it aloud:

And the word of Jehovah came unto him, saying, Arise, get thee to Zarephath, which belongeth to Sidon, and dwell there: behold, I have commanded a widow there to sustain thee. So he arose and went to Zarephath; and when he came to the gate of the city, behold, a widow was there gathering sticks: and he called to her, and said, Fetch me, I pray thee, a little water in a vessel, that I may drink. And as she was going to fetch it, he called to her, and said, Bring me, I pray thee, a morsel of bread in thy hand. And she said, As Jehovah thy God liveth, I have not a cake, but a handful of meal in the jar, and a little oil in the cruse: and, behold, I am gathering two sticks, that I may go in and dress it for me and my son, that we may eat it, and die. And Elijah said unto her, Fear not; go and do as thou hast said; but make me thereof a little cake first, and bring it forth unto me, and afterward make for thee and for thy son. For thus saith Jehovah, the God of Israel, The jar of meal shall not waste, neither shall the cruse of oil fail, until the day that Jehovah sendeth rain upon the earth. And she went and did according to the saying of Elijah: and she, and he, and her house, did eat many days. The jar of meal wasted not, neither did the cruse of oil fail, according to the word of Jehovah, which he spake by Elijah.

A young man nearby transcribed every word I spoke. A small group of Egyptians who listened to it all waited until morning. Then Al Biqa and I continued our journey home. The warmth and honor of U's family humbled me. We hid our tears, but our hearts swelled when we departed.

The Cavern

We came upon a silent cavern which was bitterly cold because the sun had never reached into its entrance since it was sunken so deep into the earth. Our trek homeward shadowed the footsteps of Elijah. Perhaps he had been guiding us through the treacherous landscape. As I tried to wrap my head around the notion that Elijah took sanctuary in the same cavern, Al Biqa and I took shelter there. When I met Elijah at the end of his life he revealed many secrets, and one of them was about his time in that cave. Forty days alone he had spent there, broken and discouraged—but God never left him. As he explained to me, God spoke to him in a whisper in that very cave in which my friends and I now hid. God cradled him with food, water and encouragement. In his solitude he was made anew by God. I tried to imagine what it was like to have a conversation with YHWH. It occurred to me that the name Elijah means "YHWH is my God." I shivered in delight at the thought. When I think back to all the peril we faced in the wilderness, every step might have been our last, but our pain and suffering were erased and forgotten by the blowing sand which, I now realized, was the work of God's breath.

The cavern, which concealed our tracks, was in a mountainous region called Horeb. Horeb was crossable only with beasts of burden. It was a dangerous mission, all the more so when carrying supplies. We were not the only ones who were protected from peril; even the men who fought for Shalmaneser received blessing in the form of victory, but all attained by bloodshed. The miracles I've have witnessed by YHWH reveals he works with individuals to accomplish his goals.

Many times I thought about the purpose of miracles in my home, and when I saw Elijah again I had a clearer grasp or ordinary events. They were, in fact, miracles.

In the cavern, my knees dug into the sandy rock. There was not even a level place to rest. Cold moisture surrounded us. One would normally assume it was a cavern of misery—but it was really a cavern of God's revelation. Even ten thousand Assyrian men would never find this secret place. God gives shelter and comfort for those to whom he chooses to reveal himself. He can control the food supply, the streams of water, the breezes... He can soften a steep hill, flatten the tallest peak, and bring life to a barren soul. I had seen it.

During our trek, Horeb's mountains were altered by the hand of God—flattened to help us accomplish our objective and keep us from death. Outside were six men with wagons full of supplies, and my friend Al Biqa was in good spirits.. He said he could smell the sea. "Yes, that is the Hinder Sea, Al Biqa," I confirmed, as I tended to him in the partially-covered wagon. The rough terrain wobbled my frail friend as we moved along. I knew our journey together had made it clear to all of us that there was hope. Our goodbye was short, as the men joined another caravan that might hasten the trip to Egypt. As I walked into Zarephath, a boy spoke out from behind me: "Are you hungry?" I turned around and told the young man that yes, indeed, I was hungry.

He Never Died

I've been home for eight years now. Through the yellow grass on my way home from an errand I see my mother, my brother, and my brother's wife. I have taken a beautiful woman as my wife. She's been helping my nephews and nieces gather material to repair the roof. We all live together now, and because of this we feel safe. I watch my son and his cousins laugh, and it puts my heart at ease. A baby crying in the distance brings my wife comfort. We have made it. Like Elijah, we prevailed. Through all his tests and near-death experiences at the hands of enemies, Elijah was invigorated by God, who consistently calmed his heart and soothed his soul. Like him, my family and I were fortunate that the trauma and pain of past times have melted away.

Many people are lost to a world that has abandoned God. Some never find a path to peace of the heart. We can hardly blame them. Ahab and his wife are no more, and every new king chooses the same path of destruction and merciless rule—but they have to learn the hard way.

We pray that those with good hearts and deep faith will never leave this earth without the opportunity to learn from a man like Elijah. It takes a man like Elijah to enter one's life, but also a woman like my mother. The spark of life deep in my mother's heart had opened the door for him.

In the afternoon, alone and far afoot in the fields, an old man comes toward me. He has sliver beard, copper skin, and large eyes full of wisdom. I know it is Elijah. We walk toward each other and weep with joy. I was just eleven the last time Elijah and I spoke, but he expresses to me that God had never stopped watching my mother and me. I tell him that my wife will be elated to see him, but he responds that his time to see God has come. We sit on a fallen tree trunk and he reveals many secrets about my journey through the war of Qarqar.

Elijah exudes wisdom and kindness. His duties for the next few days are to instruct fifty of his students at Jordan, and to then pass the mantle to another man of God, whose name is Elisha.

"Our time together was one of hope," Elijah says. "God united us for a purpose, so those who lack faith will come to believe."

"How will our time together help people believe in God?" I ask.

"God will relate the stories of our lives. It will be written in the greatest doctrine for all future generations, until the moon is no more."

"Who will write this?"

"Many unnamed and named. Kings and prophets, men and women."

Elijah tenderly puts his hand on my chin and raises my head to look into my eyes.

"We are not like the sands of the desert, to be forgotten," he says. "Those souls who fell to the sword and famine, their pain is a warning to humanity to obey God. Even with my presence in your home, there was calamity. But we all learned our lessons. God can raise the dead, unlock a torrent in a baron wilderness, and use our lives to inspire humanity."

I ask him if he had ever brought someone back to life.

"You were the only one in my ministry that I had the privilege to resurrect," he says.

I had never heard that word—resurrect.

"There will be more miracles," he continues. "Show mercy, Jonah. Show mercy and kindness, graciousness and firmness when God's sovereignty is under attack. You will have a stronger family, a peaceful life from this day on. This is what God has assured me."

He hands me a small piece of bread.

"I have kept this since the first day I met your mother. I never ate the bread she gave me that day. It was her last morsel of food."

"Why did you did not eat it?" I ask

"It was a test. A test not for me, but for your mother."

I tell him I understand.

"This morsel of wheat is more valuable than gold. Your mother's faith in face of death—yours and hers—is one of the miracles of which I speak. Since that day I have never encountered faith quite like hers. My apprentice Enoch and our fifty students are steadfast warriors for YHWH, and sometimes even they pale in comparison to your mother."

The Boy from Zarephath

"Do they know our story," I ask, "Enoch and your fifty students?"

"Yes, they do, Jonah. Women like Jezebel chased us into hiding, and men like Ahab hindered blessings upon a nation. As I search for followers I speak of ancient followers named Moses and Noah. Yes, a widow from Zarephath and her faithfulness to God is what inspires my new students."

"Do they know our names?"

"Like Moses and Noah, God has hidden their glory, God wants us to believe in what we cannot see."

"Faith," I sigh.

"Yea, faith," Elijah whispers in response. "Many people worship gods that are merely cold illusions. They have large ceremonies to these gods, only to be met with inaction."

The sun sinks behind us.

"Can you stay tonight with us, Elijah?"

"My time to enter a new dimension is near," he responds "I will go tonight back to my students."

I embrace him.

"How will I know you went to our God?"

"Twenty four moons from now," Elijah says, "look to the heavens with your family for a fire in the clouds. Then you will know I have ascended to our creator." He goes back to the tall grass. "You have made the sovereign Lord happy," he says—and then disappears.

Elijah's Lessons

Elijah had sat me down as a boy and instilled in me wisdom and foresight that I kept close to my heart forever. To Elijah I was pure innocence. That's what he told me.

One day, early in the afternoon, he told mother and me to stay quiet, for he heard military men knocking over pottery and stomping through our neighbor's garden. The men were either drunk or looking for someone in particular. Elijah feared more for our safety than his, and told mother to douse the flame on the stove. He kept his ear to the front door. It was strange for these men to be looking for those who refused to worship Baal at this time of day. The evenings were typically their hunting times, when the glow from cooking flames and fireplaces made it easy to see others without being seen themselves. Sometimes the men left carrying family members, and mothers and fathers wept. Back then, every part of life was a fight for survival. Lack of food, water, and safety drove many into madness.

In that season of drought, years ago, Elijah sat across from me at the dinner table and asked me questions—questions that helped him understand my strengths and weaknesses. First he asked if I was frightened by those drunk men who were in service only to the king.

"No, Elijah," I said. "Why do you ask? Why should I fear anything when I am guarded by you and by my mother? It would be silly if anyone of those men confronted you."

"You are a brave boy," Elijah smiled.

The war at Qarqar was more than a decade ago. I love to watch my children run free in the grass and the field, playing and doing their chores. When I close my eyes, I remember the gentle wrinkles around Elijah's eyes, the smile on U's face in the mist of chaos, and Al Biqa's long hair wrapped around his face like a warm blanket. And what I will truly never forget are the words I heard when I made it back from that incredible journey years earlier:

"You are home, my son."

The End

The Boy from Zarephath

Credits

1. Holy Bible American Standard Version – New & Old Testaments: E-Reader Formatted ASV w/ Easy Navigation

2. Names of cities researched from:
   Kraeling, E. G. H. (1918). *Aram and Israel the Aramaeans in Syria and Mesopotamia.* Eugene, OR: Wipf and Stock.

   Bryce, T. (2014). *Ancient Syria a three thousand year history.* New York, NY: Oxford University Press.

3. Cover photo credit: Salajean Media

4. Cover designed by East 4th Productions LLC

The Boy from Zarephath

The League

Adad-idri of Damascus

Adunuba'li of Shiana

Ahab of Israel

Ammon

Arabian Tribe

Arvad

Irkana

Irhuleni of Hamath

Musri

Que

Ushana

Water

Orontes River

Euphrates River

Hinder Sea: Mediterranean Sea

The Boy from Zarephath

The Boy from Zarephath